SAINSBURY'S RECIPE LIBRARY

WINTER
PUDDINGS

SAINSBURY'S RECIPE LIBRARY

WINTER PUDDINGS

SALLIE MORRIS

CONTENTS

Published exclusively for J Sainsbury plc
Stamford House Stamford Street
London SE1 9LL
by Martin Books
Simon & Schuster Consumer Group
Grafton House, 64 Maids Causeway
Cambridge CB5 8DD

ISBN 0 85941 833 2
First published 1986
Paperback edition 1992
© Woodhead-Faulkner (Publishers) Ltd 1992
All rights reserved
Printed and bound by Butler & Tanner, Frome, Somerset

INTRODUCTION

Winter puddings are part of our heritage—something particularly British. I think most of us find a beautifully made pudding hard to resist—though we certainly wouldn't want to eat one every day! This collection is perfect for family weekend meals and special occasions, probably the only occasions most of us have a pudding. It includes many old favourites—like Bread and Butter Pudding and Rice Pudding—and lots of new ideas, as well as some from overseas.

Puddings are not as popular now as they once were—probably because we've been told they're not good for us. But they don't have to be stodgy, sweet and unhealthy. The wide variety of fresh fruits now readily available all year round can be used as the base for many unusual and delicious desserts. Many kinds of dried fruits are now also widely available. These too can be turned into tasty puddings, which will provide you with iron, calcium and valuable vitamins. Add nuts and you add essential minerals.

Making steamed or sponge puddings or pastries inevitably means using sugar. If possible, use natural sugars, rather than refined white, e.g. honey, molasses, muscovado, or unrefined cane sugar. If a recipe uses dried fruits, you can cut down on sugar as they are naturally sweet.

To provide your family with a pudding which is reasonably healthy, and which you will enjoy making and they will enjoy eating, is a challenge to your imagination and creativity. While there are some 'naughty' treats for you to indulge in, this book should provide you with enough ideas to find the right pudding to suit every occasion. I do hope you and your family enjoy them as much as mine have—but not every day, please!

NOTES

Ingredients are given in both metric and imperial measures. Use either set of quantities but not a mixture of both in any one recipe.

All spoon measurements are level:
1 tablespoon = one 15 ml spoon
1 teaspoon = one 5 ml spoon.

Ovens should be preheated to the temperature specified.

Eggs are standard size 3 unless otherwise stated.

Basic recipes are marked with an asterisk and given in the reference section (pages 76–9). Increase or decrease the basic quantities in proportion to obtain the amount required.

TARTS, FLANS AND PIES

There is often confusion over what is a tart, flan, pie or plate pie. This chapter includes some of each and detailed instructions are given below for the correct rolling, cutting, shaping, lining and covering procedures.

A tart is a pastry-lined case, sometimes baked blind (see below) before being filled.

A flan is a pastry case with a thicker, higher rim. It is traditionally made in a flan ring placed on a baking sheet or a loose-based flan tin, but nowadays is often made in a ceramic flan dish. It is baked blind (see below) before being filled.

Traditionally, a pie should be made in an oval dish. The dish is filled with fruit and covered with a pastry crust, fluted round the edge.

A plate pie has a pastry top and bottom, filled with fruit. It is best made on a metal plate and then slipped onto a serving plate while still hot.

The ceramic dishes popularly used for flans are usually quite thick and it helps the pastry to cook if you place the dish on a hot baking sheet in the oven.

TO MAKE A TART
1. Roll out the pastry on a floured surface to a round about 5 cm (2 inches) larger than the pie plate.
2. Place in the plate and ease in to fit. Trim away excess pastry and cut into shapes. Brush the edge of the tart with water and arrange the pastry shapes around the edge.
3. Fill and bake as instructed in individual recipes.
For a lattice top, line the dish as above, and trim the pastry level with the edge. Roll the trimmings into a long strip and cut into pieces 0.5–1 cm (¼–½ inch) wide, to fit across the dish. Brush the edge of the tart with water and lay the strips criss-cross over the filling, pressing onto the pastry edge to seal.

TO LINE A FLAN RING, LOOSE-BASED FLAN TIN OR FLAN DISH
1. Roll out the pastry on a floured surface to a round about 5 cm (2 inches) larger than the flan ring, tin or dish.
2. Place the flan ring, if using, on a baking sheet. Lift the pastry carefully over the rolling pin and place over the ring, tin or dish.
3. Carefully ease in the pastry to fit, without creasing. Press the pastry onto the flutes if using a fluted ring or dish, or firmly to the side of a plain ring or tin.
4. Roll the rolling pin over the top of the flan to make a neat edge, then trim away the excess pastry. Bake and fill as instructed in recipes.

TO BAKE BLIND
1. Cover the pastry base with a round of greaseproof paper. Fill with ceramic beans, or dried beans or peas, to weigh down and keep the paper in place.
2. Bake in a preheated oven, 200°C/400°F/Gas Mark 6, for 15 minutes. Remove the paper and beans, and flan ring if using.
3. If the pastry case is to have an uncooked filling, return to the oven for 5–10 minutes, until the pastry is firm and cooked through. Leave to cool, then fill.

TO MAKE A PLATE PIE

1. Divide the pastry in half and roll out each piece on a floured surface to a round 2.5–5 cm (1–2 inches) larger than the pie plate.
2. Place one piece in the plate, easing to fit and covering the rim. Trim the edge and brush with water. Spoon in the filling.
3. Cover with the remaining pastry round, pressing down firmly to seal.
4. Mark the edges with the back of a knife, pressing with the back of a forefinger at the same time to crimp together.
5. Brush with beaten egg or milk if you wish and bake as instructed in recipes.

TO COVER A TRADITIONAL PIE

1. Roll out the pastry on a lightly floured surface into a shape about 2.5 cm (1 inch) larger than the pie dish. Cut round the inverted empty dish.
2. Cut the remaining pastry into a strip the same width as the rim of the dish.
3. Brush the rim with water and position the pastry strip. Press down lightly and brush with water.
4. Place a pie funnel or inverted egg cup in the centre and spoon the filling into the dish.
5. Carefully lay the lid over the rolling pin and lift on top of the pie, without stretching. Press down evenly to seal and trim off excess pastry.
6. With the forefinger of one hand resting on top of the pie, use the back of a knife to flake the edges to seal.
7. Scallop the edge at 1 cm (½ inch) intervals, using the forefinger pressed on the pastry and the knife held vertically.
8. Make a small hole in the centre and decorate with the trimmings, if you wish.
9. Brush with beaten egg or milk if you wish and bake as instructed in recipes.

MOTHER'S RHUBARB PIE

250 g (8 oz) shortcrust or rough puff pastry*	*50 g (2 oz) sugar, or to taste*
750 g (1½ lb) rhubarb, chopped	*2 tablespoons water*
¼–½ teaspoon ground ginger	*beaten egg or milk to glaze (optional)*

Serves 4–6
Preparation time:
20 minutes, plus making pastry
Cooking time:
25–30 minutes
Freezing:
Recommended at end of stage 2

1. Cut out a pastry lid to fit a 1.2 litre (2 pint) pie dish (see above). Place a pie funnel or upturned egg cup in the dish.
2. Mix together the rhubarb, ginger, sugar and water and spoon into the dish. Cover with the lid and finish as described above.
3. Place the dish on a baking sheet. Bake in a preheated oven, 200°C/400°F/Gas Mark 6, for shortcrust pastry, or 220°C/425°F/Gas Mark 7, for rough puff pastry, for 25–30 minutes, until the pastry is golden and the filling cooked through.
4. Serve hot with Custard Sauce (page 79) or cream.

COX'S APPLE PIES

The addition of a wedge of cheese is a Yorkshire idea.

500 g (1 lb) Cox's apples,
peeled, cored and sliced
1–2 tablespoons sugar
grated rind (optional) and
juice of ½ lemon
2 tablespoons water

350 g (12 oz) rough puff
*or shortcrust pastry**
milk to glaze
TO SERVE:
small wedges of Stilton or
Lancashire cheese

Makes 18
Preparation time:
20 minutes, plus
making pastry
Cooking time:
15–20 minutes
Freezing:
Recommended at
end of stage 3

1. Place the apples, sugar to taste, lemon rind if using, lemon juice and water in a pan, cover and cook for 10–15 minutes, until softened. Leave to cool.
2. Roll out the pastry on a lightly floured surface. Cut out 7.5 cm (3 inch) rounds to line 18 tartlet tins, then cut out eighteen 6 cm (2½ inch) rounds for the lids.
3. Divide the filling between the pastry-lined tins. Dampen the edge of one lid at a time and use to cover each tartlet. Make a hole in the centre of each.
4. Brush with milk and bake in a preheated oven, 220°C/425°F/Gas Mark 7, for 15–20 minutes.
5. Remove from the tins, slightly lift the tops at one side and pop in the cheese. Serve warm.

GRAPE PLATE PIE

350 g (12 oz) shortcrust
   pastry*
40 g (1½ oz) plain flour
25 g (1 oz) caster sugar
500 g (1 lb) plump black
   or green grapes, halved
   and seeded

juice of 1 small lemon
25 g (1 oz) butter, cut into
   small pieces
milk to glaze (optional)

1. Roll out the pastry as described on page 8 and use one piece to line a 25 cm (10 inch) pie plate.
2. Sift together the flour and sugar. Place the grapes in a shallow bowl. Sprinkle half the flour and sugar over the pastry case and the other half over the grapes.
3. Drizzle the lemon juice over the grapes and leave for a few minutes, then arrange in the pastry case. Dot with the butter.
4. Cover with the lid and finish as described on page 8. Use the pastry trimmings to make miniature bunches of grapes and lay on top (see picture).
5. Bake in a preheated oven, 200°C/400°F/Gas Mark 6, for 25–30 minutes.
6. Serve warm or cold with smatana or Greek strained yogurt.

Serves 8
Preparation time:
25 minutes, plus
making pastry
Cooking time:
25–30 minutes
Freezing:
Not recommended

NORFOLK TREACLE TART

An old favourite which never goes out of fashion. Measure the syrup in a bowl as suggested, or lightly dust the scale pan with flour and pour on the syrup—it will then slide out into a bowl leaving the scale pan clean.

*350 g (12 oz) wholemeal
   pastry**
*200 g (7 oz) golden syrup
   or a mixture of syrup
   and black treacle*
*40 g (1½ oz) butter or
   margarine*

1 egg, beaten
*40 g (1½ oz) fresh brown
   or white breadcrumbs*
grated rind of 1 lemon
1–2 teaspoons lemon juice
*50 g (2 oz) chopped mixed
   peel (optional)*

Serves 6–8
Preparation time:
25 minutes, plus
making pastry
Cooking time:
About 30 minutes
Freezing:
Recommended;
open freeze at end
of stage 3

1. Line a 23 cm (9 inch) metal pie plate with the pastry (see page 6). Cut a lattice top as described and set aside.
2. Weigh an empty bowl and leave on the scales. Pour in the syrup and add the butter or margarine. Place the bowl over a pan of simmering water until the butter has melted. Remove from the heat and stir in the remaining ingredients. Leave to cool.
3. Pour into the pastry case and cover with the lattice top (see page 6). Use any remaining pastry to make small shapes or balls and press onto the ends of the lattice.
4. Bake in a preheated oven, 190°C/375°F/Gas Mark 5, for about 30 minutes or until the filling is cooked and the pastry is crisp.
5. Serve this treacle tart—hot or cold—on its own or with single cream or smatana.

YORKSHIRE CURD TART

Traditionally the curds were made from the first milk of a newly calved cow. Use any small cutter or a small, sharp knife to make the pastry shapes for the edge; overlap them to hold the filling in the centre.

*250 g (8 oz) rough puff
   pastry**
FOR THE FILLING:
*227 g (8 oz) carton curd
   cheese*
*113 g (4 oz) carton
   cottage cheese*

1 tablespoon caster sugar
50 g (2 oz) currants
grated rind of 1 lemon
*1 teaspoon baking
   powder*
1 egg (size 1), beaten
*¼ teaspoon grated
   nutmeg to sprinkle*

1. Line a 25 cm (10 inch) metal pie plate with the pastry (see page 6). Roll out the trimmings into a long strip and cut into 2.5 cm (1 inch) diamonds. Dampen the pastry edge, arrange the pastry shapes attractively round the edge and prick the base.
2. Chill for 15 minutes, then bake blind (see page 6) in a preheated oven, 220°C/425°F/Gas Mark 7, for 15 minutes. Remove from the oven and lower the temperature to 190°C/375°F/Gas Mark 5.
3. Meanwhile, prepare the filling. Blend the cheeses and sugar together, then add the remaining ingredients.
4. Pour into the pastry case, sprinkle with the nutmeg and return to the oven for 20–30 minutes, until set.
5. Serve hot or warm, with fresh fruit.

Serves 6–8
Preparation time: 30 minutes, plus making pastry
Cooking time: 35–45 minutes
Freezing: Not recommended

BALMORAL TART

250 g (8 oz) wholemeal or
    shortcrust pastry*
50 g (2 oz) margarine
50 g (2 oz) caster sugar
25 g (1 oz) ground
    almonds
50 g (2 oz) stale cake
    crumbs or 3 trifle
    sponges, crumbled

2 eggs, beaten
50 g (2 oz) glacé cherries,
    halved, or candied peel
1 teaspoon grated lemon
    rind
icing sugar to dust

Serves 6–8
Preparation time:
30 minutes, plus
making pastry
Cooking time:
30 minutes
Freezing:
Recommended at
end of stage 4

1. Line a 23 cm (9 inch) pie plate with the pastry (see page 6). Roll out the trimmings into a long strip and cut into decorative shapes. Dampen the pastry edge and place the shapes on top.
2. Cream the margarine and sugar together until light and fluffy. Add the almonds and cake crumbs, then work in the beaten eggs.
3. Set aside 3 glacé cherries or a few pieces of peel. Mix the rest with the lemon rind. Stir into the mixture.
4. Spoon the prepared filling into the pastry case.
5. Bake in a preheated oven, 200°C/400°F/Gas Mark 6, for 30 minutes. Dust with icing sugar and decorate with the reserved halved cherries or peel. Serve hot or warm, with smatana if you wish.

TARTE AUX PRUNEAUX

250 g (8 oz) prunes
225 ml (7 fl oz) Madeira
    or red wine
250 g (8 oz) rich shortcrust
    pastry*
125 g (4 oz) marzipan or
    whole blanched
    almonds
50 g (2 oz) redcurrant jelly

FOR THE CRÈME
    PÂTISSIÈRE:
1 egg, separated, plus
    1 yolk
1/2 teaspoon vanilla
    essence
50 g (2 oz) caster sugar
25 g (1 oz) plain flour,
    sifted
25 g (1 oz) cornflour
400 ml (14 fl oz) milk

1. Place the prunes and Madeira or wine in a casserole dish, cover and leave overnight.
2. Cook in a preheated oven, 150°C/300°F/Gas Mark 2, for 50 minutes or until plump. Remove with a slotted spoon and set aside to cool; reserve the juice.

3. Meanwhile, line a 20 cm (8 inch) loose-based flan tin with the pastry and bake blind (see page 6).

4. To make the crème pâtissière, place the egg yolks, vanilla essence, sugar, flour, cornflour and a quarter of the milk in a bowl and beat well.

5. Bring the remaining milk to the boil, cool for 2–3 minutes, then pour onto the creamy mixture.

6. Transfer to a clean pan and heat gently, stirring, until the mixture thickens and just comes to the boil; set aside. Whisk the egg white until stiff, then fold in. Leave to cool, then spoon into the flan case placed on a serving plate.

7. Remove the stones from the prunes with care and fill the cavity with a piece of marzipan or an almond. Arrange on top of the crème pâtissière.

8. Place the redcurrant jelly and 4 tablespoons of the reserved juice in a pan and heat gently until melted, then bring just up to boiling point. Drizzle over the top of the flan and leave to set.

9. Serve cold, with whipped or pouring cream.

Serves 6
Preparation time:
1 hour, plus
soaking prunes
and making pastry
Cooking time:
50 minutes
Freezing:
Not recommended

Illustrated on
page 17

FRENCH PEAR FLAN

Use the grated pastry trimmings, if you have any, or flaked almonds to give an attractive finish to this flan.

250 g (8 oz) wholemeal or rich shortcrust pastry*
450 ml (¾ pint) white wine or pressed pear juice
5 William pears, peeled and halved
2 eggs
25 g (1 oz) plain flour, sifted

50 g (2 oz) caster sugar
25 g (1 oz) butter or margarine
½ teaspoon vanilla or almond essence
25 g (1 oz) ground almonds
25 g (1 oz) flaked almonds (optional)

Serves 8
Preparation time:
40 minutes, plus making pastry
Cooking time:
20 minutes
Freezing:
Not recommended

Illustrated below right: Tarte aux Pruneaux (page 14)

1. Line a 23 cm (9 inch) loose-based flan tin with the pastry and bake blind (see page 6) for 15 minutes.
2. If there are any pastry trimmings, wrap in clingfilm and place in the coldest part of the refrigerator or freezer until required.
3. Meanwhile prepare the filling. Place the wine or pear juice in a large pan and bring to the boil.
4. Remove the core from each pear half and place, cut side down, in the pan. Spoon over some of the liquid, cover and cook gently for 5 minutes or until almost tender. Carefully lift out the pears with a slotted spoon and set aside.
5. Measure the cooking liquid and make up to 300 ml (½ pint) with water if necessary. Return to the pan and bring to the boil.
6. Beat the eggs and flour together until smooth, then pour on the boiling cooking liquid, stirring. Return to the pan and bring to the boil, stirring, until the sauce is smooth and thickened.
7. Add the sugar, butter or margarine and essence and leave to cool.
8. Spoon half of the custard into the pastry case. Arrange the pear halves on top. Sprinkle with half of the ground almonds, then top with the remaining custard and ground almonds.
9. Using a coarse grater, grate any pastry trimmings over the flan; alternatively sprinkle with the flaked almonds.
10. Return to the oven for 20 minutes until tinged golden brown. Serve warm.

PUMPKIN PIE

This pie was introduced to the New World by early colonists and has now been adopted as a national dish. Pumpkins, with their rich, orange-coloured flesh, are at their best around Hallowe'en.

500 g (1 lb) pumpkin
25 g (1 oz) butter, softened
pinch of salt
250 g (8 oz) shortcrust or
*   wholemeal pastry**
3 eggs
75 g (3 oz) light brown soft
*   sugar*
3 teaspoons plain flour

½ teaspoon each ground
*   ginger, nutmeg and*
*   cinnamon*
170 g (6 oz) can
*   evaporated milk, or*
*   equivalent in single*
*   cream*
15 g (½ oz) pecan nuts or
*   walnuts, halved*

Serves 6–8
Preparation time:
45 minutes, plus
making pastry
Cooking time:
45 minutes
Freezing:
Not recommended

1. Peel the pumpkin, remove the seeds and cut the flesh into 1 cm (½ inch) cubes.
2. Place in a pan with the butter and heat gently for 15–20 minutes, shaking the pan occasionally, until tender.
3. Mash or work in a food processor or blender until smooth, but not *too* smooth. Add the salt and leave to cool.
4. Meanwhile, line a 23–25 cm (9–10 inch) flan ring with the pastry and bake blind (see page 6) for 15 minutes. Remove from the oven and lower the temperature to 190°C/375°F/Gas Mark 5.
5. Beat the eggs and sugar together; add the pumpkin.
6. Sift in the flour and spices, then stir in the evaporated milk or cream.
7. Pour into the prepared flan case and return to the oven for 45 minutes or until set.
8. Arrange the nuts on top and serve warm or cold (not chilled) with single cream or smatana.

FRESH LEMON FLAN

A wonderfully fresh taste to round off a meal. You could use small oranges in the same way if they better complement your menu.

2 lemons
125 g (4 oz) caster sugar
175 g (6 oz) shortcrust or
*   rich shortcrust pastry**
3 eggs, beaten

50 g (2 oz) butter or
*   margarine, cut into*
*   small pieces*
fresh bay leaves or
*   angelica to decorate*

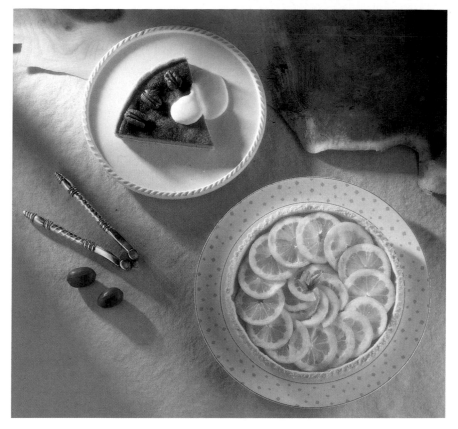

1. Cut 1 of the lemons into paper thin slices and place on a large plate. Sprinkle with 50 g (2 oz) of the sugar and leave for several hours or overnight.

2. Line a 20 cm (8 inch) loose-based flan tin with the pastry and bake blind (see page 6) for 15 minutes. Remove from the oven and lower the temperature to 180°C/350°F/Gas Mark 4.

3. Meanwhile, whisk the eggs with the remaining sugar, then add the butter or margarine.

4. Place the bowl over a pan of simmering water and stir until well blended and beginning to thicken.

5. Add the grated rind and juice of the remaining lemon and cook for 2 minutes. Leave to cool slightly.

6. Pour into the prepared flan case and return to the oven for 10 minutes. Leave to cool.

7. Just before serving, cover the surface neatly with the lemon slices and pour over the syrup which has collected.

8. Decorate with bay leaves, or angelica cut to represent leaves. Serve with Greek yogurt or single cream.

Serves 6
Preparation time: 50 minutes, plus making pastry and standing time for lemon
Cooking time: 10 minutes
Freezing: Not recommended

CHRISTMAS MERINGUE FLAN

*350 g (12 oz) rich or
    shortcrust pastry**
500 g (1 lb) mincemeat
*284 ml (10 fl oz) carton
    soured cream*

2 eggs, separated
grated rind of 1 lemon
*50 g (2 oz) ground
    almonds*
125 g (4 oz) caster sugar

Serves 8
Preparation time:
30 minutes, plus
making pastry
Cooking time:
30 minutes
Freezing:
Not recommended

1. Line a 23–25 cm (9–10 inch) flan ring with the pastry (see page 6).
2. Spoon in the mincemeat and bake in a preheated oven, 200°C/400°F/Gas Mark 6, for 20 minutes. Lower the temperature to 150°C/300°F/Gas Mark 3.
3. Meanwhile, blend the soured cream with the egg yolks, lemon rind and ground almonds.
4. Just before taking the flan out of the oven, whisk the egg whites until stiff. Whisk in half of the sugar, then whisk in the rest. Transfer to a nylon piping bag fitted with a star nozzle, if you wish.
5. Spoon the cream mixture over the mincemeat, then pipe or spoon the meringue on top. Return to the oven for 30 minutes. Serve warm or cold.

POLISH CHEESECAKE

*300–350 g (10–12 oz)
    wholemeal or shortcrust
    pastry**
*2 × 227 g (8 oz) cartons
    skimmed milk soft cheese*
125 g (4 oz) caster sugar
1 egg, plus 1 white

50 g (2 oz) butter, softened
*25 g (1 oz) plain flour,
    sifted*
25 g (1 oz) currants
25 g (1 oz) sultanas
*½ teaspoon vanilla
    essence*

Serves 6
Preparation time:
45 minutes, plus
making pastry
Cooking time:
About 45 minutes
Freezing:
Not recommended

1. Line an 18 cm (7 inch) square shallow tin with the pastry and bake blind (see page 6) for 15 minutes. Remove from the oven and lower the temperature to 180°C/350°F/Gas Mark 4.
2. Meanwhile, cut a lattice top from the pastry trimmings (see page 6) and set aside.
3. Blend the cheese with the sugar and egg, then work in the butter, flour, fruit and vanilla essence.
4. Whisk the egg white until stiff, then fold into the mixture. Pour into the pastry case and cover with the lattice top (see page 6).
5. Return to the oven for about 45 minutes, until set and lightly browned. Serve warm or cold.

SICILIAN CHESTNUTS

Marsala—a sweet dessert wine—has been produced in Sicily for over a hundred years and enhances perfectly the flavour of the chestnuts. If unobtainable, use a red wine such as Chianti or Burgundy and add a little more sugar.

750 g (1½ lb) fresh
chestnuts or 500 g (1 lb)
dried chestnuts
50–75 g (2–3 oz)
demerara sugar

600 ml (1 pint) Marsala or
medium red wine
1 large orange
4 tablespoons caster sugar

Serves 6–8
Preparation time:
35 minutes, plus soaking time if using dried chestnuts
Cooking time:
30 minutes
Freezing:
Not recommended

1. If using fresh chestnuts, cut off the tops with a sharp knife. Place a few chestnuts at a time in a pan of boiling water for 2–3 minutes. Remove with a slotted spoon and peel.
2. If using dried chestnuts, soak in cold water to cover for 5–6 hours, drain and use as fresh.
3. Place the chestnuts and demerara sugar in a clean pan, preferably flameproof enamelled or glass; use the larger amount of sugar if you are going to use a medium red wine.
4. Stir well, pour in the wine, cover and simmer over a gentle heat for 30 minutes or until just tender. Transfer to a serving dish, using a slotted spoon. Reserve the wine.
5. Meanwhile, pare a long strip from the orange with a potato peeler, then shred finely. Place in a sieve and pour over boiling water.
6. Place the caster sugar and 4 tablespoons water in a pan and heat gently, stirring, until dissolved. Add the orange shreds and cook for 3–4 minutes, stirring occasionally. Leave to cool.
7. Bring the reserved wine to the boil and cook rapidly for 3–5 minutes, until reduced and thickened. Pour over the chestnuts and sprinkle with the orange shreds.
8. Serve hot, warm or cold, with crème fraîche or Greek strained yogurt.

DATE AND WALNUT PUDDING

This pudding may not win any prizes for looks but wait until you taste it—revealed under the date and walnut topping is a delicious rich sauce.

150 g (5 oz) chopped stoned dates
125 ml (4 fl oz) warm milk
75 g (3 oz) caster sugar
125 g (4 oz) plain flour, sifted
2 teaspoons baking powder
75 g (3 oz) chopped walnuts
125 g (4 oz) light brown soft sugar

50 g (2 oz) butter or margarine
450 ml (3/4 pint) boiling water
FOR THE WINE FOAM SAUCE (optional):
300 ml (1/2 pint) white wine
1 egg
2 teaspoons caster sugar

Serves 6–8
Preparation time: 20 minutes, plus soaking time
Cooking time: 30–40 minutes
Freezing: Not recommended

1. Place the dates in a large bowl, pour over the milk and leave to soak for 30 minutes.
2. Stir in the caster sugar, flour, baking powder and walnuts. Turn into a well buttered 25 cm (10 inch) ceramic flan dish and place on a baking sheet.
3. Blend the brown sugar, butter or margarine and boiling water together and pour over the top. Bake in a preheated oven, 190°C/375°F/Gas Mark 5, for 30–40 minutes until firm. Remove from the oven and leave to stand for at least 10 minutes.
4. Serve warm with the wine foam sauce (see below) or pouring cream.
5. To make the sauce, warm the wine until just comfortable when tested with a finger.
6. Whisk the egg and sugar together, then whisk in the wine in a thin stream until light and frothy. Use at once.

DATE TART

175 g (6 oz) gingernuts, crushed
50 g (2 oz) margarine, melted
175 g (6 oz) chopped stoned dates
6 tablespoons water

1/4 teaspoon bicarbonate of soda
2 teaspoons gelatine, soaked in 6 tablespoons water
grated rind and juice of 1 lemon
1 egg white

1. Set aside 1–2 tablespoons of the larger biscuit crumbs for decoration. Mix the rest with the margarine. Press onto the base of a 20 cm (8 inch) ceramic flan dish and bake in a preheated oven, 180°C/350°F/Gas Mark 4, for 12 minutes. Leave to cool.

2. Meanwhile, place the dates, water and bicarbonate of soda in a pan and cook until the dates are soft and the mixture is like a purée.

3. Heat the gelatine gently until dissolved, then stir into the mixture with the lemon rind and juice. Chill for about 1 hour, until just beginning to set.

4. Whisk the egg white until stiff, then fold into the date mixture. Spoon into the prepared flan case and chill for at least 1 hour.

5. Sprinkle with the reserved crumbs and serve with Greek strained yogurt.

Serves 6
Preparation time: 30 minutes, plus chilling
Cooking time: 12 minutes
Freezing: Not recommended

VARIATION
Replace the biscuit crumb case with a 20 cm (8 inch) baked pastry case, either homemade (see page 6) or bought. Sprinkle the filling with a few crushed gingernuts.

ROYAL ALMOND CUSTARDS

284 ml (10 fl oz) carton
  single cream
2 large egg yolks (size 1)
25 g (1 oz) caster sugar
50 g (2 oz) ground
  almonds

FOR THE MERINGUE:
2 large egg whites (size 1)
125 g (4 oz) caster sugar
15 g (½ oz) flaked
  almonds

Makes 4
Preparation time:
45 minutes
Cooking time:
55 minutes
Freezing:
Not recommended

1. Pour the cream into a bowl and place over a pan of boiling water. Heat until the cream just reaches boiling point, then remove and cool slightly.
2. Beat the egg yolks, sugar and ground almonds together, then blend in the cream. Divide between 4 ramekins.
3. Cook in a preheated oven, 180°C/350°F/Gas Mark 4, for 30 minutes. Remove from the oven and lower the temperature to 170°C/325°F/Gas Mark 3.
4. Whisk the egg whites until stiff, then whisk in 2 teaspoons of the sugar. Whisk in the remaining sugar, half at a time.
5. Transfer the meringue to a nylon piping bag fitted with a star nozzle and pipe on top of the puddings.
6. Spike with the almonds, return to the oven and cook for 25 minutes. Serve hot, warm, or cold.

WINTER FRUIT SALAD

A no-cook winter fruit salad—the tea has a delightful flavour which blends beautifully with the fruit; replace the tea with apple, pear, or mango juice, for a sweeter result.

250 g (8 oz) packet mixed dried fruits
250 g (8 oz) dried apricots
250 g (8 oz) dried figs
125 g (4 oz) Muscatel raisins
1.2 litres (2 pints) cold jasmine tea made with 2 tablespoons tea

4 tablespoons rosewater
2 bananas
rind of 1 lemon, pared and shredded
25–50 g (1–2 oz) almond halves
25–50 g (1–2 oz) pistachio or pine nuts

1. Place the dried fruits in a bowl and pour over the tea and rosewater. Leave for 1½ days, stirring once.
2. Slice the bananas and add to the salad with the shredded lemon rind. Leave for a few more hours.
3. Sprinkle with the nuts, and serve with crème fraîche, whipped cream or Greek strained yogurt.

Serves 8–10
Preparation time: 20 minutes, plus soaking
Freezing: Not recommended

PRUNE SOUFFLÉ

250 g (8 oz) pitted prunes
50 g (2 oz) demerara or
    light brown soft sugar
2 tablespoons brandy
200 ml (7 fl oz) white wine
50 g (2 oz) butter or
    margarine

40 g (1½ oz) plain flour,
    sifted
3 eggs, separated, plus
    1 white
1 tablespoon granulated
    sugar

Serves 6
Preparation time:
30 minutes, plus
soaking time
Cooking time:
About 1 hour
Freezing:
Not recommended

1. Place the prunes, brown sugar, brandy and wine in an ovenproof casserole dish and leave to soak overnight.
2. Cover and cook in a preheated oven, 150°C/300°F/Gas Mark 2, for about 30 minutes, until plump. Strain the fruit, reserving the liquid, and chop fairly finely. Measure the reserved liquid and make up to 300 ml (½ pint) with water, if necessary.
3. Melt the butter or margarine in a pan, stir in the flour and gradually add the reserved liquid. Remove from the heat and add half of the prunes and then the egg yolks one at a time.
4. Butter the side and base of a 1.2 litre (2 pint) soufflé dish and sprinkle with the granulated sugar. Place the remaining chopped prunes in the dish.
5. Whisk the egg whites until fairly stiff, then fold 2 tablespoons into the mixture to lighten. Fold in the rest.
6. Turn into the dish, cover with an upturned bowl and leave in a warm place for up to 1 hour.
7. Cook in a preheated oven, 190°C/375°F/Gas Mark 5, for 30 minutes, until well risen.
8. Serve immediately, with single cream if you wish.

PRALINE ICE CREAM

FOR THE PRALINE:
125 g (4 oz) loaf or
    granulated sugar
4 tablespoons water
125 g (4 oz) blanched and
    split almonds

FOR THE ICE CREAM:
4 eggs, separated
few drops vanilla essence
75 g (3 oz) icing sugar,
    sifted
284 ml (10 fl oz) carton
    whipping cream

1. To make the praline, place the sugar and water in a heavy-based pan and heat gently, stirring, until the sugar has dissolved. Bring rapidly to the boil; do not stir, but watch until a rich caramel forms.

2. Stir in the almonds and continue to cook until they begin to brown, then pour immediately onto a well oiled baking sheet and leave to set.

3. Break into pieces, then place in a food processor or blender, or crush between greaseproof paper with a rolling pin, to make a fine powder. Set aside until required or store in a screw-top jar.

4. To make the ice cream, beat the egg yolks and vanilla essence together.

5. Whisk the egg whites until stiff, then whisk in 1 tablespoon of the icing sugar. Whisk in the remaining icing sugar, half at a time.

6. Whip the cream until light and fluffy, then fold into the egg white mixture with the egg yolk mixture.

7. Fold in the praline, turn into a rigid freezerproof container and freeze for 4–6 hours or until firm.

8. Allow to soften at room temperature for 20–25 minutes before serving so the full praline flavour can be enjoyed.

Serves 6–8
Preparation time:
35 minutes
Freezing time:
4–6 hours

COCONUT ICE CREAM WITH GINGER SYRUP

This recipe orginates from Southeast Asia where fresh coconut is used and the ice cream is often served in the coconut shell; desiccated coconut gives a comparable flavour. If you wish to make the ice cream in advance, remove from the freezer at least an hour before serving to give it time to soften.

2 coconuts or 500 g (1 lb)
unsweetened desiccated
coconut
1.2 litres (2 pints) boiling
water
397 g (14 oz) can
condensed milk
pinch of salt

FOR THE GINGER SYRUP:
125 g (4 oz) muscovado or
molasses sugar
200 ml ($^1/_3$ pint) water
2.5 cm (1 inch) piece fresh
root ginger, peeled and
halved

Serves 8
Preparation time:
45–55 minutes,
depending on type
of coconut used
Freezing:
Recommended for
ice cream only
Freezing time:
About 5 hours

1. If using fresh coconuts, take each one and tap all over the surface with a hammer; then split by giving a sharp blow to the crown (between the 'eyes'). Discard the clear liquid and peel away the brown outer husk. Grate the coconut flesh coarsely: you should have 500 g (1 lb).
2. Place the fresh or desiccated coconut in a food processor or blender, pour in about 900 ml (1½ pints) of the water and work for 20–30 seconds, until smooth; do this in 2 batches if necessary. Pour into a large bowl.
3. Stir in the remaining water and leave until cool.
4. Line a sieve with a large square of muslin and place in a bowl. Spoon in a quarter of the coconut, gather up the muslin and squeeze to extract as much milk as possible. Discard the spent coconut.
5. Repeat with the remaining blended coconut.
6. Stir in the condensed milk and salt. Turn into a shallow freezerproof container and freeze for 2 hours.
7. Stir well, then return to the freezer until just firm round the edges. Stir well or beat in a food processor. Return to the freezer for about 2 hours or until just firm.
8. Meanwhile, prepare the syrup. Place the sugar and water in a pan.
9. Bruise each piece of ginger with the end of a rolling pin to release the juices. Add to the pan.
10. Heat gently, stirring, until the sugar has dissolved, then simmer, uncovered, for 5 minutes.
11. Scoop the ice cream into glass dishes. Serve the syrup hot or cold, in a separate bowl.

CARIBBEAN BANANA FLAMBÉ

1 orange
50 g (2 oz) dark brown
*   soft sugar*
6 tablespoons rum

4 bananas, halved
*   lengthways*
little ground cinnamon or
*   grated nutmeg*

Serves 4
Preparation time:
10 minutes
Cooking time:
5 minutes
Freezing:
Not recommended

1. Grate the rind from half of the orange and squeeze the juice from the whole fruit.
2. Blend the sugar, orange juice and 3 tablespoons of the rum together in a large pan.
3. Add the bananas and cook for 5 minutes, spooning over the juice occasionally.
4. Sprinkle with the orange rind and cinnamon or nutmeg. Warm the remaining rum, pour over the bananas and ignite.
5. Serve hot or cold, with cream or ice cream.

GRAPEFRUIT SNOW

2 grapefruit
200 ml (7 fl oz) water
1 envelope gelatine

125 g (4 oz) sugar
2 egg whites

Serves 6
Preparation time:
30 minutes, plus
chilling
Freezing:
Not recommended

1. Pare the rind from one of the grapefruit and set aside.
2. Cut both grapefruit in half, squeeze the juice and set aside.
3. Place 4 tablespoons of the water in a small pan and sprinkle on the gelatine. Leave for a few minutes to soften.
4. Place the remaining water and the sugar in a pan and heat gently until dissolved, then bring to the boil and boil for 2 minutes. Leave to cool.
5. Heat the gelatine gently until dissolved. Add to the grapefruit juice, then add the cooled syrup. Turn into a container and freeze for 1–1½ hours, until lightly frozen. Turn into a bowl and whisk until of an even texture.
6. Meanwhile, shred and blanch the reserved grapefruit rind (see Lemon Velvet, step 4, page 34).
7. Whisk the egg whites until stiff, then carefully fold in the grapefruit mixture. Turn into a pretty glass or soufflé dish, or individual glasses or dishes, and chill until required. Decorate with the grapefruit shreds.

PAW-PAW SALAD

The rich orange-coloured flesh of the paw-paw seems to radiate sunshine; serve on vine leaves, if available, for an exotic touch.

*1 paw-paw, weighing
    about 300 g (10 oz)
1 lime*

*lemon-scented geranium
    leaves to decorate
    (optional)*

**Serves 2
Preparation time:**
10 minutes
Freezing:
Not recommended

1. Peel the paw-paw thinly, then cut in half and scoop out the seeds with a teaspoon.
2. Slice evenly lengthways into strips and arrange on 2 individual flat plates.
3. Cut the lime in half and squeeze the juice from one half over the paw-paw; cut the other half into thin slices and use to decorate, with the lemon-scented geranium leaves, if you have any. Serve immediately.

LEMON VELVET

This pudding never sets firm like ice cream, so can be served almost straight from the freezer. It's memorable with fresh raspberries or strawberries.

*8 egg yolks
250 g (8 oz) caster sugar
1 large lemon*

*284 ml (10 fl oz) carton
    whipping cream, lightly
    whipped
150 ml (¼ pint) water*

**Serves 8
Preparation time:**
30 minutes
Freezing time:
About 4 hours

1. Whisk the egg yolks and caster sugar together until pale and creamy.
2. Pare the lemon rind and set aside. Squeeze the juice and whisk into the creamed mixture. Fold in the cream, then pour into a rigid freezerproof container and freeze for 2 hours.
3. Turn into a chilled bowl and whisk again until smooth and velvety. Return to a dry container, cover, seal and freeze until firm.
4. Meanwhile, shred the reserved lemon rind very finely. Place in a pan, cover with the water and bring to the boil. Cook for 3 minutes; drain and set aside on kitchen paper.
5. To serve, scoop the lemon velvet into glass dishes and sprinkle with the shredded lemon rind.

ORANGE SHERBET

The freshly squeezed orange juice now available in so many supermarkets is perfect for this refreshing sweet.

175 g (6 oz) sugar
175 ml (6 fl oz) water
juice of 2 lemons
600 ml (1 pint) freshly
*   squeezed orange juice*

2 tablespoons Cointreau
*   or Drambuie*
TO DECORATE (optional):
orange or kumquat slices
bay leaves

Serves 6
Preparation time:
20 minutes
Freezing time:
4–6 hours

1. Place the sugar and water in a pan and heat gently, stirring, until dissolved. Bring to the boil and boil for 2 minutes. Leave to cool.
2. Add the lemon and orange juices, pour into a rigid freezerproof container and freeze for 1–2 hours, until mushy.
3. Turn into a chilled bowl and beat until smooth, or work in a food processor. Beat in the liqueur.
4. Place in a clean container, cover, seal and freeze until firm.
5. Transfer to the refrigerator 20 minutes before serving to soften. Scoop into individual stemmed glasses or glass dishes to serve.
6. Decorate with orange or kumquat slices and bay leaves if you wish.

MANGO BRÛLÉE

Choose firm mangoes without bruises. If not quite ripe, wrap in newspaper and leave in the airing cupboard until required. The rich orange flesh has a wonderfully exotic flavour which you will love in this really simple recipe.

2 very large mangoes, weighing just over 500 g (1 lb) each

rind of ½ small orange 150 g (5 oz) muscovado sugar

1. Using a sharp knife, cut each mango horizontally from the stem end, shaving over the flat stone on one side. Turn cut side down and repeat on the other side. Remove the stone, scoop out half the flesh with a spoon into a food processor or blender and work until smooth. Add the orange rind and blend well.
2. Cut the remaining mango flesh into small pieces.
3. Pour the purée into 8 ovenproof ramekin dishes and top with the chopped fruit. Chill for at least an hour or until required.
4. Just before serving sprinkle with the sugar, then place under a preheated hot grill for 4–5 minutes, until the sugar melts and slightly caramelizes.
5. Leave to cool slightly for 2–3 minutes before serving.

Serves 8
Preparation time: 25 minutes, plus chilling
Cooking time: 4–5 minutes
Freezing: Not recommended

TROPICAL FRUIT SALAD

75 g (3 oz) sugar
300 ml (½ pint) water
2.5 cm (1 inch) piece fresh
  root ginger
1 small paw-paw, peeled
  and deseeded
1 ripe mango
2 kiwi fruit, peeled and
  sliced

2 passion fruit
2 bananas, sliced
125 g (4 oz) kumquats,
  sliced
125 g (4 oz) grapes, halved
  and seeded
1 guava, peeled and sliced

Serves 8
Preparation time
20 minutes, plus
chilling
Freezing:
Not recommended

1. Place the sugar and water in a pan and heat gently until dissolved.
2. Bruise the ginger with the end of a rolling pin and add to the pan. Bring to the boil and boil for 2 minutes. Leave to cool.
3. Meanwhile, cut the paw-paw into pieces and place in a serving bowl.
4. Remove the flesh from the mango as described in Mango Brûlée (page 37). Dice the flesh and add to the bowl with the kiwi fruit.
5. Cut the passion fruit in half and scoop out the fleshy seeds into the bowl with a teaspoon.
6. Add the bananas, kumquats, grapes and guava to the bowl and fold in gently.
7. Strain over the syrup, cover and chill until required.
8. Serve in individual glass dishes, with crisp dessert biscuits if you prefer.

TWENTY-FOUR HOUR SALAD

Best made up a day ahead, as its name suggests. The sharpness of the pineapple and the sweetness of the marshmallow complement each other well.

3 egg yolks
2 tablespoons caster sugar
2 teaspoons distilled white
  vinegar
pinch of salt
2 tablespoons pineapple
  juice or lemon juice
25 g (1 oz) butter
284 ml (10 fl oz) carton
  double cream, whipped

1 small fresh pineapple,
  chopped, or 432 g
  (15¼ oz) can pineapple
  pieces in natural juice,
  drained
125 g (4 oz) marsh-
  mallows, chopped
4 passion fruit

1. Place the egg yolks, sugar, vinegar, salt, pineapple or lemon juice and butter in the top of a double boiler or in a basin placed over a pan of simmering water and whisk until smooth and thickened. Cool, then chill in the refrigerator for 30 minutes.

2. Fold in the cream, pineapple and marshmallows.

3. Reserve 1 passion fruit to decorate, cut the remainder in half, and use a teaspoon to scoop the flesh and seeds into the salad. Mix well, turn into a bowl, cover with clingfilm and chill for 24 hours.

4. Divide between individual glass dishes. Halve the reserved passion fruit and spoon a little of the flesh and seeds over each dessert before serving.

Serves 6–8
Preparation time: 30 minutes, plus chilling
Freezing: Not recommended

GRANNY'S FAVOURITES

This collection of recipes includes all-time favourites—the so-called 'nursery puddings' that Granny used to make so superbly. Not many families eat steamed puddings nowadays, but the few that I have included are sure to bring back memories.

BAKED CUSTARD

Smooth and velvet-textured custard is good hot, warm or cold. Try serving it with the Winter Fruit Salad (page 27).

3 eggs
600 ml (1 pint) milk,
warmed to blood heat

25 g (1 oz) caster sugar
few drops vanilla essence
little grated nutmeg

Serves 4
Preparation time:
5 minutes
Cooking time:
About 45 minutes
Freezing:
Not recommended

1. Whisk the eggs, then stir in the warmed milk. Strain into a greased 900 ml (1½ pint) ovenproof dish. Stir in the sugar and vanilla essence, then sprinkle with nutmeg.
2. Place the dish in a roasting tin and pour in water to come halfway up the side of the dish.
3. Bake in a preheated oven, 170°C/325°F/Gas Mark 3, for 45 minutes or until set. Serve hot, warm or cold.

LEMON DELIGHT

The delight in this recipe comes from finding a creamy lemon sauce under the sponge topping.

125 g (4 oz) butter or soft
margarine
150 g (5 oz) caster sugar
finely grated rind and
juice of 2 lemons

4 eggs, separated
125 g (4 oz) self-raising
flour, sifted
350 ml (12 fl oz) milk

Serves 8
Preparation time:
25 minutes
Cooking time:
About 45 minutes
Freezing:
Not recommended

1. Cream the butter or margarine, sugar and lemon rind together until light and fluffy.
2. Beat in the egg yolks, then gradually beat in the flour and milk. Stir in the lemon juice.
3. Beat the egg whites until stiff, then fold into the mixture. Turn into a greased 1.75 litre (3 pint) ovenproof dish and place in a roasting tin half-filled with water.
4. Bake in a preheated oven, 180°C/350°F/Gas Mark 4, for about 45 minutes, until set and pale golden brown.

EVE'S PUDDING

500–625 g (1–1¼ lb)
cooking apples or pears,
peeled, cored and sliced
50 g (2 oz) granulated or
light brown soft sugar
1–2 tablespoons water
grated rind and juice of
½ lemon

125 g (4 oz) butter or soft
margarine
125 g (4 oz) caster sugar
2 eggs, beaten
175 g (6 oz) self-raising
flour, sifted
2 tablespoons milk
little icing sugar to sprinkle

Serves 4–6
Preparation time:
25 minutes
Cooking time:
35–45 minutes
Freezing:
Not recommended

1. Place the apples or pears, granulated or brown sugar, water, lemon rind and juice in a greased 1.2 litre (2 pint) ovenproof dish.
2. Cream the butter or margarine and caster sugar together until light and fluffy.
3. Beat in the egg with a little of the flour, then fold in the remaining flour with the milk to make a soft dropping consistency.
4. Spoon on top of the fruit, level the surface with the back of the spoon, and bake in a preheated oven, 190°C/375°F/ Gas Mark 5, for 35–45 minutes, until the sponge is risen and the fruit tender.
5. Sprinkle with icing sugar and serve hot with Greek yogurt or single cream.

VARIATION
Use plums or rhubarb instead of apples or pears: stone plums and cut rhubarb into 2.5 cm (1 inch) pieces. Omit the lemon rind and juice and replace with ½–1 teaspoon ground cinnamon if using plums, or ground ginger for rhubarb; sift in with the flour.

SAUCER PANCAKES

50 g (2 oz) butter
50 g (2 oz) caster sugar
1 teaspoon grated lemon
rind (optional)
2 eggs, beaten lightly
50 g (2 oz) plain flour
pinch of salt

300 ml (½ pint) milk
½ teaspoon vanilla
essence (optional)
FOR THE TOPPING:
175 g (6 oz) raspberries or
other soft fruit
15–25 g (½–1 oz) sugar

1. Cream the butter and sugar together until light and fluffy. Add the lemon rind, if using, then beat in the egg a little at a time.

2. Sift the flour and salt together, then fold into the mixture alternately with the milk to make a batter; it may look curdled but this does not matter. Add the vanilla essence, if using.

3. Divide the mixture between 5 or 6 greased ovenproof saucers or 18 cm (7 inch) foil plates and bake in a preheated oven, 190°C/375°F/Gas Mark 5, for 15–20 minutes, until fluffy and pale golden.

4. Meanwhile, make the topping: place the raspberries and sugar in a pan and warm together gently until the sugar has dissolved.

5. Spoon on top of the pancakes and serve immediately.

Serves 5–6
Preparation time:
20 minutes
Cooking time:
15–20 minutes
Freezing:
Not recommended

VARIATIONS

1. Top the pancakes with jam and whipped cream.

2. Cream together 175 g (6 oz) curd cheese, 1 egg yolk, 15 g (½ oz) butter, 1 tablespoon sugar and ½ teaspoon grated lemon rind, until light. Use as a topping.

QUEEN OF PUDDINGS

150 g (5 oz) fresh white or
brown breadcrumbs
75 g (3 oz) caster sugar
grated rind of 1 lemon
600 ml (1 pint) milk

50 g (2 oz) butter or
margarine
2 eggs (size 2), separated
3–4 tablespoons raspberry
jam, warmed

Serves 6
Preparation time:
35 minutes
Cooking time:
45–50 minutes
Freezing:
Not recommended

1. Place the breadcrumbs, 25 g (1 oz) of the sugar and the lemon rind in a bowl.
2. Place the milk and butter or margarine in a pan, bring to the boil, then pour over the breadcrumbs. Leave to cool for 15 minutes, then stir in the egg yolks.
3. Turn the mixture into a greased 1.2 litre (2 pint) ovenproof dish and bake in a preheated oven, 180°C/ 350°F/Gas Mark 4, for just under 30 minutes, until the top looks set. Remove from the oven and lower the temperature to 150°C/300°F/Gas Mark 2.
4. Spoon the jam over the surface.
5. Whisk the egg whites until stiff, add 25 g (1 oz) of the remaining sugar and whisk again. Fold in the remaining sugar.
6. Place in a nylon piping bag fitted with a large star nozzle and pipe attractively over the jam.
7. Return to the oven for 15–20 minutes, until the meringue is pale golden. Serve hot.

CRANBERRY AND APPLE CRUMBLE

This is a Canadian-inspired recipe. Try substituting plums
for cranberries and pears for apples.

*250 g (8 oz) fresh
cranberries
6 tablespoons water
4 tablespoons granulated
sugar
500 g (1 lb) cooking
apples, peeled, cored
and sliced thinly
75 g (3 oz) plain flour*

*pinch of salt
75 g (3 oz) butter or
margarine
25 g (1 oz) skimmed milk
powder
40 g (1½ oz) rolled oats
75 g (3 oz) light brown soft
sugar
1 teaspoon ground
cinnamon*

1. Place the cranberries, water and granulated sugar in a
pan, bring to the boil and cook for 5 minutes. Leave to
cool, then place in a greased 1.5 litre (2½ pint) shallow
ovenproof dish with the apples.
2. Sift the flour and salt into a bowl and rub in the butter or
margarine until the mixture resembles coarse crumbs. Stir
in the remaining ingredients, then spoon evenly over fruit.
3. Bake in a preheated oven, 180°C/350°F/Gas Mark 4, for
25–30 minutes, until the topping is crisp and the fruit
tender. Serve hot.

Serves 6
Preparation time:
25 minutes
Cooking time:
25–30 minutes
Freezing:
Not recommended

CHOCOLATE DENVER PUDDING

A rich chocolate pudding with its own special sauce underneath—a little taste of heaven for all chocolate fans! Use a deep dish as the sauce bubbles during cooking.

50 g (2 oz) butter
3 tablespoons cocoa
  powder
75 g (3 oz) caster sugar
125 g (4 oz) plain flour
2 teaspoons baking
  powder
pinch of salt
6 tablespoons milk
¼ teaspoon vanilla
  essence

FOR THE TOPPING:
50 g (2 oz) dark brown
  soft sugar
50 g (2 oz) caster sugar
2 tablespoons cocoa
  powder
300 ml (10 fl oz) cold
  coffee, made with 2 tea-
  spoons instant coffee

Serves 4–6
Preparation time:
25 minutes
Cooking time:
40 minutes
Freezing:
Not recommended

1. Place the butter and cocoa powder in a large bowl over a pan of simmering water until melted. Stir in the sugar.
2. Sift the flour, baking powder and salt together, then beat into the mixture, with the milk and vanilla essence.
3. Turn the mixture into a deep greased 20–23 cm (8–9 inch) square or round ovenproof dish.
4. Mix together the brown sugar, caster sugar and cocoa powder and sprinkle over the top. Pour over the coffee.
5. Bake in a preheated oven, 180°C/350°F/Gas Mark 4, for 40 minutes. Serve hot or warm with cream or smatana.

RICE PUDDING WITH LEMON

A comforting pudding which goes down well with all the family, young or old. The grated lemon rind adds an interesting flavour to this old favourite.

40 g (1½ oz) pudding rice
600 ml (1 pint) milk
25 g (1 oz) sugar
grated rind of ½ lemon

little margarine or butter
TO SERVE (optional):
little lemon curd

Serves 4
Preparation time:
5 minutes
Cooking time:
About 2 hours
Freezing:
Not recommended

1. Place the rice, milk, sugar and lemon rind in a greased 900 ml (1½ pint) ovenproof dish. Stir well, then dot with margarine or butter.
2. Cook in a preheated oven, 150°C/300°F/Gas Mark 2, for about 2 hours, until creamy.
3. Serve hot, topped with a little lemon curd if you wish.

BREAD AND BUTTER PUDDING

A so-called 'nursery pudding' which, it is claimed, is one of the most popular in men's London clubs, including the restaurants of the Houses of Parliament.

25 g (1 oz) currants or
sultanas
50 g (2 oz) chopped
candied peel
3 tablespoons rum
300 ml (½ pint) milk
2 large eggs (size 1),
beaten

6 large slices buttered
bread, crusts removed,
cut into fingers
25–50 g (1–2 oz)
demerara sugar
a little grated nutmeg

Serves 4–6
Preparation time:
20 minutes, plus soaking and standing time
Cooking time:
45–55 minutes
Freezing:
Not recommended

1. Soak the currants or sultanas and peel in the rum for several hours.
2. Heat the milk almost to boiling point, remove from the heat, then whisk into the eggs.
3. Strain the fruit, reserving the rum, and set aside. Add the rum to the custard mixture.
4. Use one third of the bread to line the base of a greased 900 ml (1½ pint) ovenproof dish. Sprinkle with half of the fruit. Repeat the layers, finishing with bread slices arranged attractively on top.
5. Sprinkle with half of the sugar. Strain over the custard and leave to stand for 30 minutes.
6. Sprinkle with the remaining sugar and nutmeg.
7. Place the dish in a roasting tin half-filled with water.
8. Bake in a preheated oven, 150°C/300°F/Gas Mark 2, for 45–55 minutes or until the pudding is just set. Serve hot.

VARIATION
Dissolve 2 teaspoons instant coffee in a little of the milk; add to the custard. Replace the candied peel with coarsely chopped walnuts.

GINGER AND SYRUP SPONGE

125 g (4 oz) self-raising
flour
1 teaspoon ground ginger
125 g (4 oz) butter or
margarine
125 g (4 oz) light brown
soft sugar

2 eggs
3 tablespoons milk
3 tablespoons golden syrup
1 teaspoon peeled and
finely chopped fresh root
ginger (optional)

1. Brush a 1.2 litre (2 pint) pudding basin with oil and cut a circle of baking parchment to fit the base.
2. Sift the flour and ginger together and set aside.
3. Cream the butter or margarine and sugar together until light and fluffy. Beat in the eggs, with a little of the flour. Fold in the remaining flour with the milk to make a soft dropping consistency.
4. Spoon the syrup and chopped ginger, if using, into the dish and cover with the sponge mixture.
5. Prepare the basin as instructed on page 52 and steam the pudding for 1¼–1½ hours. Leave to stand for 2–3 minutes, then turn out onto a warmed serving dish. Serve very hot with Custard Sauce (page 79) or pouring cream.

Serves 6
Preparation time:
25 minutes
Cooking time:
1¼–1½ hours
Freezing:
Not recommended

NIGHT AND DAY PUDDING

The name comes from the dark-as-night pudding served
with the light-as-day cream.

75 g (3 oz) butter or margarine	*50 g (2 oz) self-raising flour, sifted*
100 g (3½ oz) caster sugar	*TO DECORATE (optional):*
3 eggs, separated	*284 ml (10 fl oz) carton*
125 g (4 oz) plain chocolate, melted	*whipping cream, whipped*
125 g (4 oz) blanched almonds, chopped finely	*a few chocolate curls (see below)*

Serves 6–8
Preparation time:
30 minutes
Cooking time:
1¼–1½ hours
Freezing:
Not recommended

1. Grease a 900 ml (1½ pint) soufflé dish and line the base
with baking parchment.
2. Cream the butter or margarine and sugar together until
light and fluffy, then beat in the egg yolks. Stir in the
chocolate and almonds, then fold in the flour.
3. Beat the egg whites until stiff, then fold into the mixture. Spoon into the dish and cover as instructed on page
52. Steam for 1¼–1½ hours.
4. Leave to stand for 30 minutes until cool. Turn out onto a
serving plate, cover with whipped cream and sprinkle
with chocolate curls. Alternatively, serve hot or warm,
with pouring cream handed separately.

To make chocolate curls: Use a potato peeler to scrape
long curls from a block of chocolate which has been
standing at room temperature for 15 minutes.

PRINCE ALBERT PUDDING

Whether this pudding was ever eaten by Prince Albert or
whether he had a fondness for prunes I do not know!

175 g (6 oz) prunes, soaked overnight in 300 ml (½ pint) water	*125 g (4 oz) fine white or brown breadcrumbs*
50 g (2 oz) light brown soft sugar	*½ teaspoon baking powder*
50 g (2 oz) butter or margarine	*1 egg (size 1), separated*
50 g (2 oz) caster sugar	*175 ml (6 fl oz) milk*
	grated rind and juice of 1 lemon

1. Grease a 900 ml (1½ pint) pudding basin and cut a circle of baking parchment to fit the base.
2. Place the prunes, with their soaking liquid, and brown sugar in a pan, bring to the boil, then simmer for 30 minutes, until plump. Strain, reserving the juice, and remove stones. Place in the prepared basin.
3. Cream the butter or margarine and caster sugar together until light and fluffy. Add the breadcrumbs, baking powder, egg yolk, milk and half of the lemon rind.
4. Whisk the egg white until stiff, then fold into the mixture. Spoon into the basin.
5. Prepare the basin as instructed on page 52 and steam the pudding for 1–1¼ hours. Leave to stand for a few minutes, then turn out onto a warmed serving dish.
6. Meanwhile, boil the reserved cooking liquid for 2–3 minutes to reduce it slightly. Cool a little, then add the remaining lemon rind and the juice. Serve with the pudding.

Serves 6
Preparation time: 25 minutes, plus soaking time
Cooking time: 1–1¼ hours
Freezing: Not recommended

CHRISTMAS PUDDING

A homemade Christmas pudding is a most welcome gift —why not keep one and give two away? This is certainly my favourite recipe: it is rich, fruity and moist but the brown breadcrumbs give it a beautifully light texture. Because the mixture stands overnight before cooking there is no need to soak the fruit first.

500 g (1 lb) each raisins, sultanas and currants
250 g (8 oz) chopped mixed peel
500 g (1 lb) butter or margarine
500 g (1 lb) dark brown soft sugar
5 eggs
125 g (4 oz) clear honey grated rind and juice of 1 lemon

175 g (6 oz) self-raising flour
½ teaspoon each ground mixed spice, cinnamon, cloves and grated nutmeg
500 g (1 lb) fresh brown breadcrumbs
150 ml (5 fl oz) brandy or rum
2–3 tablespoons milk

Makes three 1.2 litre (2 pint) puddings
Preparation time: 1¼ hours, plus standing time
Cooking time: 6 hours, plus 3 hours steaming to serve
Freezing: Not recommended

1. Grease three 1.2 litre (2 pint) pudding basins and cut a circle of baking parchment to fit the base of each.
2. Mix the fruit and peel together and set aside.
3. Cream the butter or margarine and sugar together until light and fluffy. Beat in the eggs, then stir in the honey, lemon rind and juice.
4. Sift the flour and spices together, then stir into the mixture with the breadcrumbs and fruit. Stir in the brandy or rum and milk.
5. Cover the bowl with foil and leave overnight in a cool place.
6. Divide the mixture between the basins and prepare as instructed below. Steam for 6 hours.
7. Leave until cold, then cover with fresh baking parchment and foil. Store in a cool, dry place.
8. To serve, re-steam for 3 hours. Flame with brandy and serve with brandy butter or Custard Sauce (page 79).

TO COVER A PUDDING FOR STEAMING
1. Place a disc of baking parchment loosely over the pudding mixture in the basin.
2. Tear off a large square of foil and fold in half. Make a 2.5 cm (1 inch) pleat along the fold.
3. Lay the foil over the basin with the pleat centrally positioned; this will allow the pudding to rise.

4. Twist the foil under the rim of the basin firmly.

5. Tear off another long piece of foil and fold in half. Place the basin on this and use to lift in and out of the pan.

6. Place in a steamer over a pan of boiling water, or in a saucepan half-filled with boiling water, and cook for the time given in individual recipes; keep the pan topped up with boiling water during cooking.

MOCHA CHOCOLATE POTS

These wickedly rich little puddings never fail to impress. Here I have used Tia Maria coffee liqueur but you could equally well use dissolved instant coffee granules.

250 g (8 oz) dark bitter chocolate, broken into pieces
4 tablespoons water
25 g (1 oz) butter or margarine, cut into small pieces
5 egg yolks
600 ml (1 pint) milk

1 tablespoon Tia Maria, or to taste, or 1 tablespoon instant coffee granules dissolved in 2 tablespoons hot water
TO DECORATE (optional):
142 ml (5 fl oz) carton whipping cream, whipped
8–10 chocolate rose leaves (see page 64)

Makes 8–10
Preparation time: 30 minutes
Cooking time: About 45 minutes
Freezing: Not recommended

1. Place the chocolate and water in a large bowl over a pan of simmering water until melted. Cool slightly, then add the butter or margarine and stir well.
2. Beat the egg yolks and gradually stir in the milk. Stir into the chocolate mixture, then add the Tia Maria or coffee.
3. Strain into a measuring jug, then pour into 8–10 ramekin or small ovenproof dishes. Place in a roasting tin half-filled with warm water and cook in a preheated oven, 170°C/325°F/Gas Mark 3, for about 45 minutes or until just firm on top.
4. Serve cold topped with a rosette of piped cream and a chocolate rose leaf; alternatively serve warm with a little pouring cream.

VARIATION
Replace the Tia Maria or coffee with Cointreau, Grand Marnier or finely grated orange rind.

THE EARL'S ICE CREAM

There are so many interesting teas on the market now which could be used in this recipe, but try an old favourite first before experimenting with others.

2 tablespoons Earl Grey or
Lapsang Souchong tea
300 ml (1/2 pint) freshly
boiled water
5 egg yolks

125 g (4 oz) caster sugar
284 ml (10 fl oz) carton
single cream
284 ml (10 fl oz) carton
double cream, whipped

Serves 6–8
Preparation time:
20 minutes
Cooking time:
15 minutes
Freezing time:
4–6 hours

1. Infuse the tea and boiling water for a few minutes. Strain and set aside.
2. Whisk the egg yolks and caster sugar together until pale and frothy.
3. Heat the single cream gently, then gradually whisk into the egg yolk mixture with the tea.
4. Pour into a clean saucepan, or leave in the bowl and place over a pan of simmering water, and stir until the custard begins to thicken; do not boil. Leave to cool, then turn into a rigid freezerproof container and freeze for about 2 hours, until half-frozen and mushy.
5. Whisk hard, then fold in the whipped double cream. Pour back into the washed container, cover, seal and freeze until firm.
6. Transfer to the refrigerator about 1 hour before serving to soften.
7. Scoop into individual glass dishes and serve with dessert biscuits if you wish.

PORT WINE JELLY AND SPICED CREAM

This rich ruby red jelly will add a touch of grace and elegance to any dinner party or dessert trolley. It's a good alternative to Christmas pudding, too.

350 ml (12 fl oz) port (not
tawny)
2 envelopes gelatine
1 tablespoon lemon juice
125 ml (4 fl oz) water
50 g (2 oz) caster sugar

FOR THE SPICED CREAM:
284 ml (10 fl oz) carton
whipping cream
a little ground cinnamon
and grated nutmeg
25 g (1 oz) icing sugar
(optional)

1. Pour 150 ml (¼ pint) of the port into a pan, sprinkle over the gelatine and add the lemon juice. Leave for 3–4 minutes, until the gelatine has softened.
2. Add the water and sugar. Heat gently, stirring, until the sugar has dissolved.
3. Strain through a coffee filter or a sieve lined with muslin. Leave to cool slightly, then add the remaining port.
4. Pour into 4–6 individual wetted moulds or into one 600 ml (1 pint) mould and leave to set.
5. Dip each mould briefly in boiling water and turn out onto a serving plate.
6. Whip the cream, then add the spices and icing sugar, if using. Either pipe decoratively round the base of each jelly or serve separately.
7. For Christmas, top each jelly with a sprig of holly or mistletoe, or gold or silver leaf.

Serves 4–6
Preparation time: 30 minutes, plus setting time
Freezing: Not recommended

BRANDIED PEACHES

4 large yellow peaches or
nectarines, or 822 g
(1 lb 13 oz) can peach
halves in syrup, drained
2 tablespoons light brown
soft sugar (optional)
50 g (2 oz) butter

4 tablespoons brandy,
warmed
8–16 ratafia biscuits
142 ml (5 fl oz) carton
soured cream
25 g (1 oz) flaked
almonds, toasted

Serves 4
Preparation time:
10 minutes
Cooking time:
4–5 minutes
Freezing:
Not recommended

1. If using fresh peaches or nectarines, plunge into boiling water for 30 seconds. Remove with a slotted spoon and skin immediately. Cut in half and remove the stones. Spoon a little of the sugar into the cavities.
2. Melt the butter in a large frying pan and add the fruit. Pour over the brandy and set alight.
3. When the flames have died down, cook for 4–5 minutes if using fresh fruit, 2 minutes if using canned.
4. Transfer to a warmed serving dish. Place 1–2 ratafias in each peach or nectarine half, top with soured cream and sprinkle with almonds. Serve with dessert biscuits.

PLUM AND ALMOND MOUSSE

500 g (1 lb) plums, halved
and stoned
150 ml (¹/4 pint) water
50 g (2 oz) caster sugar
1 envelope gelatine
3 eggs, separated

25 g (1 oz) ground
almonds
250 g (8 oz) skimmed milk
soft cheese
flaked almonds, toasted, to
decorate

Serves 6
Preparation time:
30 minutes, plus
setting and chilling
time
Cooking time:
15 minutes
Freezing:
Not recommended

1. Place the plums, water and half the sugar in a pan. Simmer for 15 minutes, until tender. Strain, reserving juice.
2. Measure 150 ml (¹/4 pint) of the juice into a pan and sprinkle over the gelatine; set aside.
3. Meanwhile, purée the plums in a food processor or blender and set aside in a large bowl.
4. Place the egg yolks, ground almonds and remaining sugar in a heatproof bowl over a pan of simmering water and whisk until pale. Stir into the plum purée.
5. Heat the gelatine mixture until dissolved. Cool slightly, then stir in the plum mixture. Set aside for 20–30 minutes until the mixture begins to set.
6. Stir in the soft cheese. Whisk the egg whites until stiff and fold in. Spoon into 6 individual dishes and chill until set. Decorate with toasted almonds.

CRANBERRY AND ORANGE SOUFFLÉ

Freshly-squeezed orange juice gives this soufflé a wonderful fresh flavour.

40 g (1½ oz) butter or margarine
40 g (1½ oz) plain flour
450 ml (¾ pint) freshly-squeezed orange juice
2 tablespoons granulated sugar

125 g (4 oz) cranberries, chopped roughly
25 g (1 oz) caster sugar
3 eggs, separated, plus 1 white
little icing sugar to sprinkle

Serves 6
Preparation time:
30 minutes
Cooking time:
30 minutes
Freezing:
Not recommended

1. Melt the butter or margarine in a pan, stir in the flour and cook for a few minutes.
2. Remove from the heat and gradually blend in the orange juice. Return to the heat and stir until smooth and thick. Leave to cool.
3. Meanwhile, coat the inside of a buttered 1.5–1.7 litre (2½–3 pint) soufflé dish with a tablespoon of the granulated sugar. Stir the other tablespoon into the cranberries and spoon into the soufflé dish.
4. Place the orange mixture in a large bowl and stir in the caster sugar and egg yolks.
5. Whisk the egg whites until stiff. Fold 2 tablespoons into the orange mixture to lighten it, then fold in the remainder. Spoon on top of the cranberries.
6. Place on a baking sheet and bake in a preheated oven, 190°C/375°F/Gas Mark 5, for 30 minutes.
7. Sprinkle lightly with icing sugar and serve immediately, on its own or with pouring cream.

ANZAC CHRISTMAS PUDDING

Your family or guests will be more than delighted with this 'down under' pudding

15 g (½ oz) butter, melted
25 g (1 oz) shortbread biscuits, crushed
284 ml (10 fl oz) carton whipping cream
6 tablespoons mincemeat
2 tablespoons brandy
600 ml (1 pint) vanilla ice cream

125 g (4 oz) each red and green glacé cherries, halved
40 g (1½ oz) chopped almonds
25 g (1 oz) pistachio nuts (optional)
few drops almond essence

1. Brush a 1 litre (1¾ pint) bombe mould or pudding basin with the melted butter and coat with the biscuit crumbs. Place in the freezer.

2. Whip the cream until it holds its shape, then fold in the mincemeat and brandy. Spoon into the mould and freeze for about 20 minutes.

3. Press the partly frozen cream to the side of the mould or basin with a spoon, leaving a deep hollow in the centre. Return to the freezer for 1 hour.

4. Soften the vanilla ice cream and add 50 g (2 oz) each of the red and green cherries, the almonds, pistachios if using, and almond essence. Spoon into the hollow in the mould, cover, seal and freeze until firm.

5. About 45 minutes before serving, dip the mould into very hot water and turn out onto a serving dish. Place in the refrigerator.

6. Decorate the pudding with the reserved cherry halves and a sprig of holly if wished. Cut into wedges with a sharp knife to serve.

Serves 8
Preparation time:
30 minutes
Freezing time:
6 hours

PROFITEROLES WITH CHOCOLATE SAUCE

*1 quantity Choux Pastry**
284 ml (10 fl oz) carton
whipping cream

142 ml (5 fl oz) carton
double cream
1 quantity Chocolate
*Sauce**

Serves 8–10
Preparation time:
25 minutes, plus
making pastry and
sauce
Cooking time:
20–25 minutes
Freezing:
Recommended;
open freeze at end
of stage 2

1. Spoon the choux pastry into a nylon piping bag fitted with a plain 1 cm (½ inch) nozzle and pipe into small mounds the size of an egg yolk on 2 lightly oiled baking sheets.
2. Bake in a preheated oven, 220°C/425°F/Gas Mark 7, for 20–25 minutes, until risen and crisp. Cut a slit in the side of each, then cool on a wire rack.
3. Mix the creams together, then whip until firm. Spoon into a clean dry piping bag fitted with a small plain nozzle and use to fill the profiteroles. Pile them up into a pyramid on a glass or china cake stand and pour over the chocolate sauce, warm or cold.

PEARS IN RED AND WHITE WINE

300 ml (½ pint) red wine
300 ml (½ pint) white
wine
600 ml (1 pint) water
350 g (12 oz) caster sugar

2 cinnamon sticks
8 cloves
12 even-sized fairly firm
Conference pears

Serves 6
Preparation time:
30 minutes, plus
chilling
Cooking time:
30 minutes
Freezing:
Not recommended

1. Pour the red and white wines into 2 separate pans. Top up each with 300 ml (½ pint) water.
2. Divide the sugar, cinnamon sticks and cloves between the pans. Bring to the boil, stirring until the sugar has dissolved.
3. Peel the pears and place half in each pan. Cover and simmer gently for 30 minutes or until tender.
4. Arrange the pears in a serving dish. Cover with clingfilm and chill until required.
5. Meanwhile, boil the cooking liquids hard until reduced to a syrup. Leave to cool.
6. Pour the white wine syrup over the pears. Serve the red wine syrup separately in a jug. Serve with single cream if you wish.

CHOCOLATE ROULADE

An all-time favourite, from France.

5 eggs, separated
175 g (6 oz) caster sugar
175 g (6 oz) plain dark
  chocolate, melted
2 tablespoons hot water

icing sugar to dust
284 ml (10 fl oz) carton
  whipping cream,
  whipped
chocolate leaves (see
  below) to decorate

Serves 6–8
Preparation time:
35 minutes, plus
standing time
Cooking time:
15–20 minutes
Freezing:
Recommended,
without chocolate
shapes

1. Line a 33 × 23 cm (13 × 9 inch) Swiss roll tin with baking parchment.
2. Whisk the egg yolks and sugar together until pale and fluffy. Stir in the melted chocolate and hot water.
3. Whisk the egg whites until stiff, then fold into the chocolate mixture.
4. Pour into the prepared tin, tipping it at the edges so that the mixture is evenly distributed.
5. Bake on the shelf above the centre of a preheated oven, 190°C/375°F/Gas Mark 5, for 15–20 minutes, until the surface is crusty and puffy. Cover with a sheet of baking parchment and a teatowel and leave for at least 8 hours.
6. Place the baking parchment on the teatowel and dust with icing sugar. Invert the roulade onto it and remove the lining paper. Trim the edges with a sharp knife.
7. Spread with two thirds of the cream then, using the baking parchment to help, roll up neatly and lift carefully onto a serving dish.
8. Decorate with remaining cream and chocolate leaves.

VARIATIONS
1. Add 75–125 g (3–4 oz) chopped after-dinner mints to the cream and use a few, halved, to decorate.
2. Add 2 tablespoons Grand Marnier and 1 teaspoon grated orange rind to the cream and decorate with shredded orange rind.

To make chocolate leaves: Rinse and dry rose leaves carefully. Using a small butter knife, spread melted chocolate evenly over the back of the leaf, taking it just to the edges. Leave to dry, chocolate side up. When set hard, carefully lift the tip of the leaf and peel away.

IDA'S APFEL STRUDEL

This popular Austrian dessert requires patience, which will be rewarded if you carefully follow this authentic recipe. The pastry can be made in a food processor.

250 g (8 oz) plain flour
pinch of salt
150 ml (¼ pint) warm
water
25 g (1 oz) white fat or
lard, cut into small
pieces
750 g (1½ lb) cooking
apples, peeled, cored
and sliced thinly
finely grated rind and
juice of 1 lemon

50 g (2 oz) sugar
½ teaspoon ground
cinnamon
50 g (2 oz) sultanas
125 g (4 oz) butter, melted
50 g (2 oz) fresh
breadcrumbs
25 g (1 oz) ground
almonds
little icing sugar to dredge
(optional)

Serves 8
Preparation time:
45 minutes, plus
standing time
Cooking time:
40 minutes
Freezing:
Not recommended

1. Sift the flour and salt into a mound on a clean worktop. Make a deep well in the centre.
2. Using a fork, whisk 1 tablespoon of the flour into the warm water.
3. Place the fat in the well, pour in the water and blend together with a palette knife to form a soft dough that peels away easily from the hands.
4. Bang the dough several times on the work surface, then knead for 5 minutes.
5. Warm a bowl and invert over the dough, cover with a towel and leave for at least 30 minutes.
6. Meanwhile, mix the apples, lemon rind and juice, sugar, cinnamon and sultanas together.
7. Place half of the melted butter in a pan and stir in the breadcrumbs. Heat gently, stirring, until golden.
8. Roll out the pastry on a floured surface into a large square, then transfer to a clean teatowel well dredged with flour. Roll out a little more.
9. Slip your hands underneath the dough and gently draw out from the edges until it covers the tea towel without breaking; any holes must be patched.
10. Brush the surface with a little melted butter. Cover with the apple mixture, breadcrumbs and ground almonds, leaving a 3.5 cm (1½ inch) border all round.
11. Fold in the 2 shorter sides and the edge nearest to you then, using the cloth, roll over loosely like a Swiss roll. Place on a greased baking sheet, seam side down, and form into a horseshoe shape.

12. Brush with half the remaining melted butter and bake in a preheated oven, 200°C/400°F/Gas Mark 6, for 20 minutes. Brush with the remaining butter. Lower the temperature to 190°C/375°F/Gas Mark 5, and bake for 20 minutes.

13. Serve hot or cold, dredged with icing sugar and accompanied with cream if you wish.

GREEK YOGURT DESSERT

Greek strained yogurt has become immensely popular —you just have to taste it to know why! Here it is served in tall glasses, drizzled with clear honey and with fresh figs set on the side. When lychees are in season, serve instead of the figs.

480 g (1 lb 1 oz) carton
Greek strained yogurt
2–4 tablespoons clear
honey

4–8 fresh figs or 12–16
lychees

Serves 4
Preparation time:
10 minutes, plus
chilling
Freezing:
Not recommended

1. Divide the yogurt between 4 stemmed glasses and drizzle over the honey to taste. Chill thoroughly.
2. To serve, place each glass on a small plate with 1–2 figs or 3–4 lychees.

DANISH APPLE TRIFLE

1 kg (2 lb) cooking apples,
peeled, cored and sliced
75 g (3 oz) caster sugar, or
to taste
4 tablespoons water
1 teaspoon vanilla essence
125 g (4 oz) butter
250 g (8 oz) breadcrumbs,
from a stale loaf

2–3 tablespoons sherry
125 g (4 oz) ratafias or
macaroons
TO DECORATE:
142 ml (5 fl oz) carton
whipping cream,
whipped
1–2 tablespoons
redcurrant jelly

Serves 6–8
Preparation time:
35 minutes
Cooking time:
15–20 minutes
Freezing:
Not recommended

1. Place the apples, sugar and water in a pan, bring to the boil, then cover and simmer until reduced to a pulp. Cool a little, add the vanilla essence and leave until cold.
2. Meanwhile, melt half of the butter in a frying pan, add half of the breadcrumbs and fry until crisp and brown. Spoon onto kitchen paper. Repeat with the remaining butter and breadcrumbs. Leave to cool.
3. Arrange the apple purée and breadcrumbs in alternate layers in a glass dish.
4. Sprinkle the sherry over the ratafias or macaroons and arrange a row around the edge of the dish; dot the remainder over the surface of the pudding.
5. Swirl whipped cream on top, within the row of ratafias or macaroons.
6. Warm the redcurrant jelly, then drizzle over the dessert, using a teaspoon or piping bag. Chill until required.

PASHKA

This is a rich Russian pudding which must be well refrigerated before turning out. Lining the bowl with 2 strips of baking parchment arranged in a cross eases turning out.

2 × 227 g (8 oz) cartons
  cream cheese
50 g (2 oz) caster sugar
2 egg yolks
1 teaspoon vanilla essence
1 envelope gelatine,
  soaked in 4 tablespoons
  cold water

284 ml (10 fl oz) carton
  whipping cream,
  whipped
25 g (1 oz) sultanas
25 g (1 oz) walnuts,
  chopped
75 g (3 oz) split blanched
  or flaked almonds
25 g (1 oz) angelica
8–10 walnut halves

Serves 6–8
Preparation time: 30 minutes, plus chilling
Freezing: Recommended; thaw for 5–6 hours before serving

1. Line a 1.5 litre (2½ pint) bombe mould or pudding basin with 2 strips of baking parchment.
2. Beat the cheese until soft, then beat in the sugar, egg yolks and vanilla essence.
3. Heat the gelatine gently until dissolved. Cool slightly, then stir into the creamed mixture. Fold in the cream, then the sultanas, chopped walnuts and two thirds of the almonds.
4. Turn into the prepared mould, cover and chill in the refrigerator for 6–8 hours.
5. Meanwhile, lightly toast the remaining almonds; cool.
6. To serve, turn out onto a serving plate, spike the surface with the toasted almonds and angelica, cut into diamonds, and arrange the walnut halves around the base.

AMERICAN ICE BOX CAKE

Layers of sponge and chocolate mousse combine to make this glorious American dessert. It is best made a day ahead. Decorate, then return to the refrigerator until required.

1 quantity Victoria Sponge
  *mixture**
175 g (6 oz) plain choco-
  late, broken into pieces
3 tablespoons boiling
  coffee
3 eggs, separated

2 tablespoons rum or
  brandy
TO DECORATE:
142 ml (5 fl oz) carton
  whipping cream,
  whipped
chocolate curls (see page
  50)

1. Make and bake the sponge mixture in a 33 × 23 cm (13 × 9 inch) Swiss roll tin as described. Cool on a wire rack.
2. Line a 1 kg (2 lb) loaf tin with a long strip of baking parchment to cover the base and hang over each end.
3. Place the chocolate in a food processor or blender, add the *boiling* coffee, leave for 1–2 minutes to soften, then blend for a few seconds, until the chocolate has melted. Blend in the egg yolks one at a time, then stir in the rum or brandy. Turn into a bowl and set aside to thicken slightly.
4. Meanwhile, whisk the egg whites until stiff. Fold 2 tablespoons into the chocolate mixture to lighten, then fold in the rest.
5. Cut the cake widthways into 3 pieces. Place one piece in the prepared tin and cover with half of the mousse mixture. Repeat the layers, finishing with sponge.
6. Cover with foil or clingfilm and chill for 12–24 hours.
7. Turn out onto a serving dish, pipe with the cream and decorate with chocolate curls.

Serves 8
Preparation time:
35 minutes, plus making sponge and chilling
Freezing:
Recommended

SWEDISH TOSCA APPLES

Pears, peaches or plums could be cooked in the same way.

3 cooking apples, peeled,
cored and halved
75 g (3 oz) butter or
margarine
125 g (4 oz) sugar

2 tablespoons plain flour,
sifted
4 tablespoons top of the
milk or cream
50 g (2 oz) flaked almonds

Serves 6
Preparation time:
15–20 minutes
Cooking time:
20–25 minutes
Freezing:
Not recommended

1. Place the apples round side uppermost in a well buttered ovenproof dish.
2. Place the butter or margarine, sugar, flour and milk or cream in a pan and heat gently until blended. Add the almonds and stir well.
3. Pour over the apples and bake in a preheated oven, 200°C/400°F/Gas Mark 6, for 20–25 minutes, until the apples are tender. Serve immediately, with cream.

SOUFFLÉ OMELETTE

This French dessert is ideal for a twosome.

2 eggs, separated
2 teaspoons caster sugar
few drops vanilla essence
1 tablespoon single cream
or top of the milk
15 g (½ oz) butter

3–4 tablespoons apricot
preserve
25 g (1 oz) flaked
almonds, toasted
sifted icing sugar for
sprinkling

Serves 2
Preparation time:
5 minutes
Cooking time:
4–5 minutes
Freezing:
Not recommended

1. Beat the egg yolks, sugar, vanilla essence and cream or milk together.
2. Whisk the egg whites until stiff, fold in 2 tablespoons to lighten the mixture, then fold in the rest.
3. Melt the butter in a 23 cm (9 inch) omelette or frying pan and rub round with a piece of kitchen paper.
4. Turn the mixture into the pan and cook for about 4 minutes until set, lifting at the edges with a knife to make sure that it is not cooking too quickly.
5. Place under a preheated hot grill for 1 minute.
6. Spread with the apricot preserve, sprinkle with the almonds, then fold in half. Turn onto a warmed serving plate and sprinkle with icing sugar.
7. Heat a metal skewer over a gas flame or electric ring. Holding it with an oven glove, use to score the surface. Serve immediately.

NORWEGIAN BOMBE ALASKA

Invented by an American scientist in the 19th century, the solid block of ice cream stays firm inside the meringue covering even when baked at a very high temperature in the oven. If you prefer to make your own ice cream, freeze it in a container not quite as wide as the sponge.

½ quantity Victoria	*4 egg whites*
Sponge mixture*	*125 g (4 oz) caster sugar*
350 g (12 oz) frozen	*2 × ½ litre (1 pint) blocks*
raspberries, thawed	*vanilla ice cream*

Serves 8
Preparation time:
20 minutes, plus
making sponge
Cooking time:
3–5 minutes
Freezing:
Not recommended

1. Make and bake the sponge in a 20 cm (8 inch) round sandwich tin as directed. Cool on a wire rack.
2. Place the sponge on an ovenproof plate or flan dish and cover with the raspberries and their juice.
3. Whisk the egg whites until stiff, then whisk in the sugar a tablespoon at a time. Place the ice cream on top of the raspberries.
4. Swirl the meringue over the whole pudding and place immediately in a preheated oven, 230°C/450°F/Gas Mark 8, for 3–5 minutes, until the meringue is pale golden. Serve immediately.

VARIATION
Replace the raspberries with glacé fruits, e.g. cherries, pineapple, soaked in brandy or kirsch for 3–4 hours.

PAVLOVA

An all-time favourite, named after the famous ballet dancer who captivated the New Zealanders in 1926. The outside of the meringue becomes crisp while the centre is soft and marshmallow-like. Top with cream and sliced fruit, e.g. ½ a pineapple, 250 g (8 oz) soft summer fruits, 2 kiwi fruit or nectarines, or a colourful selection of fruit.

3 egg whites	*½ teaspoon vanilla*
pinch of salt	*essence*
175 g (6 oz) caster sugar	*142 ml (5 fl oz) carton*
1 teaspoon cornflour	*whipping cream,*
1 teaspoon white distilled	*whipped*
vinegar	*fruit of your choice (see*
	above)

1. Line a baking sheet with baking parchment or grease-proof paper. Draw on a 20 cm (8 inch) round and set aside.
2. Whisk the egg whites and salt together until holding its shape, then whisk in half of the sugar.
3. Stir the cornflour into the remaining sugar, then fold into the meringue. Add the vinegar and vanilla essence, folding in gently.
4. Lightly oil the marked round. Spread the meringue on top, smooth the surface, then make a dip in the centre. Cook in a preheated oven, 150°C/300°F/Gas Mark 2, for 1 hour.
5. Transfer to a wire rack to cool, then remove the lining paper.
6. Spread the whipped cream evenly over the top and decorate with the fruit of your choice.

Serves 6–8
Preparation time:
45 minutes
Cooking time:
1 hour
Freezing:
Recommended,
without topping

SHORTCRUST PASTRY

250 g (8 oz) plain flour
pinch of salt
50 g (2 oz) each white
vegetable fat and butter
or margarine, cut into
small pieces

2–3 tablespoons cold
water

**Makes 250 g
(8 oz) quantity
Preparation time:**
10 minutes
Freezing:
Recommended

1. Sift the flour and salt into a large bowl. Rub in the fat until the mixture resembles breadcrumbs.
2. Sprinkle in the water, then stir with a round-bladed knife until the mixture begins to bind.
3. Using one hand, collect the dough into one piece and knead lightly. Set aside for 10–15 minutes if possible. If you wish to make it in advance, place in a polythene bag and keep in the refrigerator until required, but do allow to return to room temperature before rolling out.
4. Roll out on a lightly floured surface with a lightly floured rolling pin in short, even, forward strokes to the size and thickness required.

RICH SHORTCRUST PASTRY

This is a slightly richer pastry which is ideal for flans and tarts. The egg yolk and water used to bind the dough give a shorter crisp pastry which must be handled with care.

250 g (8 oz) plain flour
pinch of salt
125 g (4 oz) butter or
margarine, cut into
small pieces

25 g (1 oz) caster sugar
1 egg yolk
2–3 tablespoons cold
water

**Makes 250 g
(8 oz) quantity
Preparation time:**
10 minutes
Freezing:
Recommended

1. Sift the flour and salt into a bowl. Rub in the fat until the mixture resembles breadcrumbs. Stir in the sugar.
2. Beat the egg yolk with 1 tablespoon of the water and sprinkle over the mixture. Mix with a round-bladed knife, adding more water as necessary.
3. Bind, knead, rest and roll as for shortcrust pastry (above) and use as required.

WHOLEMEAL PASTRY

Use half wholemeal flour and half plain or self-raising flour to produce the best result. Using all wholemeal flour tends to give a slightly heavier pastry. Wholemeal flour absorbs more water, hence the extra water in the recipe.

125 g (4 oz) wholemeal flour
125 g (4 oz) plain or self-raising flour
pinch of salt

125 g (4 oz) white vegetable fat, cut into small pieces
3–4 tablespoons cold water

1. Place the wholemeal flour in a bowl and sift in the plain or self-raising flour and salt.
2. Add the fat and proceed as for shortcrust pastry. Use as required.

Makes 250 g (8 oz) quantity
Preparation time: 10 minutes
Freezing: Recommended

ROUGH PUFF PASTRY

This pastry is very straightforward to make; it is best used on the day it is made.

250 g (8 oz) plain flour
pinch of salt
1 teaspoon baking powder

150 g (5 oz) white vegetable fat, cut into tiny pieces
150 ml (¼ pint) cold water (approximately)

1. Sift the flour, salt and baking powder into a bowl. Add the fat and mix in lightly with a round-bladed knife.
2. Sprinkle over the water, then stir with the knife until the mixture almost binds together. Finish binding with one hand.
3. Roll out on a lightly floured surface into a strip 30 × 10 cm (12 × 4 inches).
4. Fold the lower third up and the top third down. Seal the edges with the rolling pin.
5. Make a quarter turn, roll out and fold in the same way twice more.
6. Set aside for at least 30 minutes before using as required.

Makes 250 g (8 oz) quantity
Preparation time: 15 minutes
Freezing: Recommended

CHOUX PASTRY

75 g (3 oz) butter   *pinch of salt*
300 ml (½ pint) water   *4 eggs, beaten*
150 g (5 oz) plain flour,
*   sifted*

**Makes a 4-egg
quantity
Preparation time:**
30 minutes
Freezing:
Recommended,
cooked, but
unfilled

1. Place the butter and water in a pan and heat gently until melted, then bring just up to boiling point. Remove from the heat and stir in the flour and salt. Beat until the mixture forms a ball; do not overheat.
2. Set the pan aside until you can comfortably hold your hand on the side of the pan.
3. Add two thirds of the egg, beating well.
4. Gradually add as much of the remaining egg as necessary, until the mixture is of piping consistency. Leave to cool, then use as required.

VICTORIA SPONGE

125 g (4 oz) butter or   *125 g (4 oz) self-raising*
*   margarine*   *   flour, sifted*
125 g (4 oz) caster sugar   *2 tablespoons milk*
2 eggs, beaten lightly

**Makes a 2-egg
quantity
Preparation time:**
20 minutes
Cooking time:
15–20 minutes
Freezing:
Recommended

1. Line two 20 cm (8 inch) sandwich tins or one 33 × 23 cm (13 × 9 inch) Swiss roll tin with baking parchment.
2. Cream the butter or margarine and sugar together until light and fluffy.
3. Add the eggs one at a time, adding a little of the flour with the second egg. Beat well.
4. Fold in the remaining flour, then the milk. Turn into the prepared tin(s).
5. Bake on the shelf above the centre of a preheated oven, 190°C/375°F/Gas Mark 5, for 15–20 minutes, until golden and leaving the side(s) of the tin(s). Cool on a wire rack.

CHOCOLATE SAUCE

This is a very useful chocolate sauce to make, as it keeps in the refrigerator without thickening. It can be used hot or cold on profiteroles, ice cream or in milk shakes.

125 g (4 oz) light brown
soft sugar
150 ml (¼ pint) water

4 tablespoons cocoa
powder
a little rum (optional)

1. Place the sugar and water in a pan and heat gently, stirring, until dissolved. Remove from the heat and whisk in the cocoa powder.
2. Return to heat and bring just up to the boil, then simmer for 1 minute.
3. Cool slightly and use, or store in a covered plastic container in the refrigerator until required.
4. Stir in a little rum if you wish.

Makes 200 ml
(⅓ pint)
Preparation time:
5 minutes
Cooking time:
4 minutes
Freezing:
Not recommended

CUSTARD SAUCE

This is a lovely custard, worthy of many of the recipes in this book. The addition of cornflour helps stabilize the sauce, preventing it from curdling.

300 ml (½ pint) milk or
single cream
1 egg, plus 1 yolk
1 teaspoon cornflour

¼ teaspoon vanilla
essence
25 g (1 oz) caster sugar or
to taste

1. Heat the milk or cream but do not boil.
2. Blend the remaining ingredients together in a basin, pour in the warm milk or cream and stir well.
3. Strain into a non-stick pan and heat gently, stirring, until thickened. If it begins to curdle, remove from the heat and keep stirring to return it to a smooth sauce.
4. Use hot or cold as desired.

Makes 300 ml
(½ pint)
Preparation time:
10 minutes
Cooking time:
5 minutes
Freezing:
Not recommended

INDEX

Photography by: Laurie Evans
Designed by: Sue Storey
Home economist: Carole Handslip
Stylist: Lesley Richardson
Illustration by: Linda Smith
Typeset by Rowland Phototypesetting Limited